Three Twentieth-Century
Dictators

by India Ruby

Table of Contents

Adolf Hitler

The year is 1935, and a man named Adolf Hitler is ruling Germany. This man has destroyed all political parties except his own. He has given himself the power to change laws and make new ones. Worst of all, he is violent and hateful—some say insane. He is making laws that will lead to the murders of millions of innocent people. Why is no one stopping him? How is he able to do this? He is able to do this because he is a dictator.

A dictator is a ruler who holds **absolute power** over a country. Dictators make laws and important decisions without the approval of other people. They are often feared and hated by the people they rule—and by people of other countries as well.

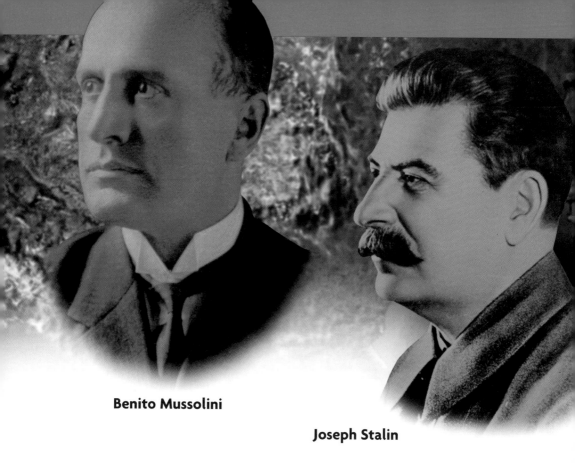

Benito Mussolini

Joseph Stalin

Adolf Hitler was one of the cruelest and most feared dictators of all time. He despised Jewish people and planned to rid Europe of them completely. Millions of Jews and other people suffered and died because of Hitler's hatred. Meanwhile, he invaded one country after another in an attempt to rule Europe. His desire for power started World War II.

Hitler was not the only dictator of the twentieth century. Benito Mussolini (buh-NEE-toh MOO-suh-LEE-nee) of Italy had dreams of conquering other countries. He joined Hitler in his attempt to take over Europe. The Soviet Union's Joseph Stalin was another power-hungry, violent ruler who made death and destruction his mission in life.

This postcard shows a happy Soviet citizen supporting Stalin. This is an example of propaganda.

How do dictators such as Hitler, Mussolini, and Stalin come to power? Many use violence to seize power and keep it. They take away people's rights and freedoms, including freedom of speech and freedom of the press. Most dictators outlaw elections. What happens to those who disagree with a dictator's methods? They end up in prison or dead.

Some dictators come to power during times of crisis. When war or poverty has weakened a country, its people are hungry, tired, and scared. That's when many future dictators start their rise to power. They make promises and tell people what they want to hear. They influence people using communication called **propaganda**. Propaganda is information designed to promote a certain cause or belief. Often the information is misleading. Eager for a strong leader to solve their problems, many people believe the propaganda. They allow the dictator to take over.

In this book you will find out about the early lives of Hitler, Mussolini, and Stalin. You will learn about the people and events that influenced them. You will discover how they came to power, and what life was like for the people they ruled. As you read this book, notice the methods that Hitler, Mussolini, and Stalin used to gain control and keep it.

Hitler (left) and Mussolini parade through Rome, Italy.

Adolf Hitler

It was January 30, 1933, and much of Germany was celebrating. Crowds gathered in the streets to cheer their new chancellor, or leader. His name was Adolf Hitler. In twelve years the world would know how wrong the German people were to trust Adolf Hitler.

Adolf Hitler was born on  April 20, 1889, in a small town in Austria. Hitler was a poor student and his bad-tempered father was deeply disappointed in his son's failures. Some say he beat his son.

At the age of 16, Hitler dropped out of high school. He liked to paint and wanted to become an artist. Although he applied twice to Vienna, Austria's Academy of Fine Arts, he couldn't pass the entrance exam.

For the next few years, young Hitler lived and painted in Vienna. He sold a few paintings for small sums in coffeehouses or on the street.

a painting
by Adolf Hitler

No one knows for certain why Hitler hated Jewish people or when this hatred began. But it was during his years in Vienna that Hitler's political beliefs began to take shape. He read books that led him to develop a deep hatred of Jewish people. He also believed that Germans were better than other people.

Hitler was an angry and troubled young man. He had big ideas that were out of touch with reality. Once he bought a lottery ticket, and was so sure he would win that he picked out an expensive apartment for himself. When he didn't win, he was furious. He blamed lottery officials and the government for cheating honest people out of their money.

Adolf Hitler

In 1914, World War I broke out. The German side fought against Great Britain, Russia, and the United States. Hitler served as a message runner in the German army and won medals for bravery.

Germany lost the war in 1919. The country was forced to give up its weapons and some of its territory. Germany also had to pay $30 billion for the damage it had caused during the war.

Like many Germans, Hitler was shocked and angry about these conditions. But he believed that he could rescue Germany from the shame of losing the war. Hitler joined the German Workers' Party. By 1921, he had become party leader. He changed the party's name to the National Socialist German Workers' Party, or the Nazi Party. He set up a private army of assault troops called the storm troops.

Meanwhile, Germany was facing serious problems. Many workers had gone on strike to demand better working conditions. Gangs fought on the streets with German military groups.

By 1923, the economy had collapsed because of inflation. During a period of inflation, money loses some value and buys less than it did before. German money had become almost worthless. People needed wheelbarrows filled with money just to buy a pound of potatoes or a loaf of bread.

These are the bombed-out buildings of a German town destroyed during World War I.

As the leader of the Nazi Party, Hitler took advantage of these problems. He had a talent for public speaking, and he gave loud, angry speeches that excited the German people. In his speeches, Hitler promised to make Germans rich and happy. He also tried to convince Germans that the Jews were to blame for the country's troubles. His speeches made crowds cheer, "Heil (HIGHL), Hitler!" This means "Hail, Hitler!"

Government officials salute Hitler.

In late 1923, Hitler saw a chance to take control of a part of Germany. He burst into a government meeting and fired a pistol into the air. Hitler called on supporters to follow him, but the takeover failed. He spent nine months in prison for the incident.

While in prison, Hitler wrote his autobiography, called *Mein Kampf* (MIGHN KAHMPF) or *My Struggle*. It described his early life and his views. In the book, Hitler claimed that Germans were a superior race of people. He wrote that Germans had a right to seize more land for themselves. He argued that Jews were to blame for most of Germany's troubles. These beliefs were not based on any facts or logic. When Hitler got out of prison, he immediately set out to build his power and that of the Nazi Party.

PRIMARY SOURCE

In *Mein Kampf*, Hitler wrote about the power of propaganda. He wrote, "The broad mass of a nation . . . will more easily fall victim to a big lie than to a small one."

In 1929, conditions in Germany became much worse when a worldwide economic **depression** began. During a depression, jobs are few and wages are low. Most people have very little money to spend. Because of this, it is hard for businesses to sell their products and services. Businesses lose money and lay off workers. Some businesses just shut down.

Millions of German people lost their jobs during this depression. The government seemed unable to solve the country's problems. Germans began to pay attention to Hitler's extreme ideas. They liked his promises to make things better. His popularity grew daily.

In the 1933 election, Hitler's Nazi Party got enough votes to win a place in the government. Hitler became chancellor. He forced the government to pass laws giving him complete power. He used his assault troops to terrorize anyone who disagreed with him. He killed or imprisoned his political opponents.

Make Connections

Think of a time in your life when someone else had control over you. How did you feel? What did you want to do?

Hitler watches Nazi assault troops pass by.

Hitler had become a dictator with evil plans. He ordered German factories to begin making weapons for war. His military used these weapons to take over Austria and Czechoslovakia (cheh-kuh-sloh-VAHK-ee-uh) in 1938. In 1939, Germany invaded Poland. This action started World War II. By 1940, Germany had invaded and taken over much of Europe.

NAZI PROPAGANDA

Joseph Goebbels (GER-buhlz) was the propaganda leader of the Nazi Party. Goebbels had total control of German media. For example, he used movies to spread the idea that Germany needed Hitler and the Nazi Party.

Meanwhile, Hitler had been increasing his **persecution**, or abuse, of Jews. In Germany, he prevented Jews from taking certain jobs. He stripped Jews of their German citizenship. He seized their businesses. He forced them to wear a yellow star to show that they were Jewish. Nazis beat and killed Jews just for being Jewish.

Finally, Hitler had Jews sent to **concentration camps**, or prison camps. There, up to 2,000 people at a time were killed in gas chambers. This was part of the Nazi policy called "The Final Solution of the Jewish Question." This policy called for the murder of every Jew who lived under German rule.

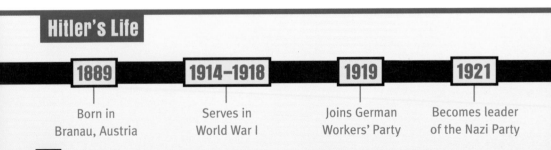

Hitler's Life

1889	1914–1918	1919	1921
Born in Branau, Austria	Serves in World War I	Joins German Workers' Party	Becomes leader of the Nazi Party

Concentration camp prisoners celebrate after being freed by the U.S. Army in 1945.

Hitler had more than 11 million people murdered in concentration camps. Six million of them were Jews. This tragic period of mass murder of Jews and others is called the **Holocaust**.

World War II raged on. In April 1945, the Soviet Union captured Berlin, the capital of Germany. The rest of the **Allies**, including the United States and Britain, had conquered Germany from the west. When Germany fell, Hitler was hiding in an underground shelter. Knowing that he was defeated, Hitler shot himself. His death marked the end of one of the most brutal dictatorships the world has ever known.

1924–1925	1933	1939	1945
Writes *Mein Kampf* in prison	Named chancellor of Germany	Invades Poland, which starts World War II	Commits suicide

Benito Mussolini

Benito Mussolini ruled as a dictator in Italy. Like Adolf Hitler, he allowed no opposition to his rule. Mussolini joined with Hitler in World War II. Both men were defeated, and died violently at war's end.

Benito Mussolini was born on July 29, 1883, near Predappio (prih-DAHP-ee-oh), Italy. In 1883, Italy was mostly a country of farmers. Although some goods were produced there at the time, Italy could not be called an industrial nation. It lagged far behind the industrial countries of western Europe. People in Italy were either rich or they were poor. Most were poor, including Mussolini's family.

Mussolini's mother was a teacher. His father was a blacksmith and a loyal supporter of **socialism**. Under socialism, the government controls businesses and industries. The people of the country share the goods and services that are produced.

the house where Mussolini was born

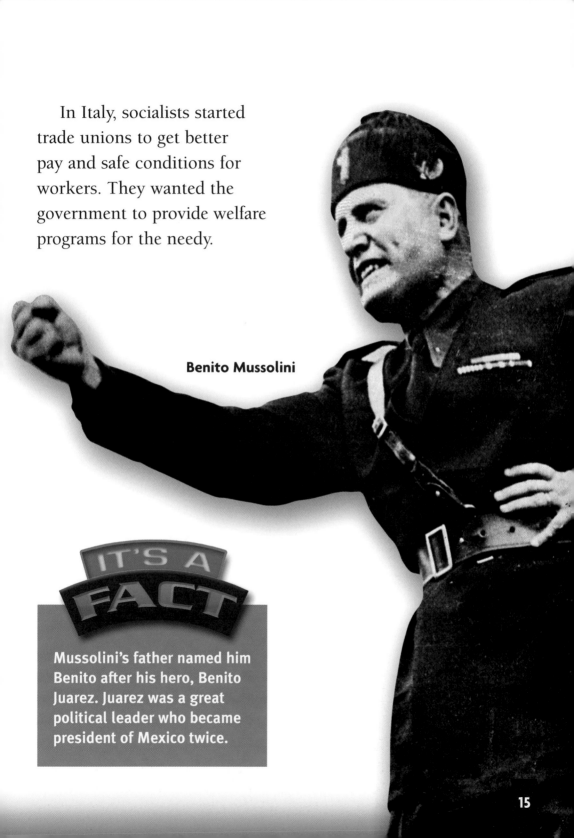

In Italy, socialists started trade unions to get better pay and safe conditions for workers. They wanted the government to provide welfare programs for the needy.

Benito Mussolini

IT'S A FACT

Mussolini's father named him Benito after his hero, Benito Juarez. Juarez was a great political leader who became president of Mexico twice.

As a boy, Mussolini was fiery and rebellious. He stole from local farmers and picked fights at school. He became an eager socialist like his father. Young Mussolini earned a teaching degree in 1901 and got a job teaching elementary school. But his bad behavior got him fired after only a year.

Mussolini at about 16 years old

Mussolini moved to Switzerland in 1902. While in Switzerland, he learned more about socialism. He was not able to find a permanent job there, but he found he had a talent for public speaking. He spoke out against religion, the government, and the military. When he suggested that Swiss workers go on strike, he was kicked out of Switzerland. He returned to Italy.

In 1905 and 1906, Mussolini served in the Italian army. Later, he worked as a teacher again, but again he was fired. In 1909, he moved to Austria where he wrote for a socialist newspaper. In Austria, he spoke out against religion and was thrown out of that country, too.

AN ANGRY BOY

Stories of Mussolini's youth note that he was hot-tempered and sometimes violent. At school, he led a student revolt against the quality of the food. He was later thrown out of school for wounding a student with a knife.

Once more Mussolini returned to Italy. In 1912, he became the editor of the Italian Socialist Party's newspaper. Then in 1914, he started his own newspaper, *Il Popolo d'Italia (eel POP-puh-loh dee-TAL-ee-uh)* or "The People of Italy."

As a young socialist, Mussolini had spoken out against war. He had even been arrested when he led an anti-war demonstration. Socialists believed that war forced workers to fight while factory owners got rich. But Mussolini's beliefs about war began to change after the start of World War I in 1914. He saw the war as a "great drama." In his newspaper, he urged Italy to join World War I. His new views got him thrown out of the Socialist Party.

Italy did enter the war in 1915. The country fought against Germany on the side of the Allies. Mussolini served in the army but left military service in 1917 after he was wounded. The Allies and Italy won World War I. But Italy received far less territory than it had been promised. Many Italians felt betrayed and were very angry.

Mussolini in his World War I uniform

By 1919, Mussolini had turned from socialism to **fascism** (FA-shih-zuhm). A fascist government tightly controls its country, often through use of force. It does not allow opposition. That year Mussolini founded the *Fasci di Combattimento*, (FAH-shee dee CAWM-baht-tee-mehn-toh) or Combat Groups. They later became the National Fascist Party. Mussolini started making plans to take over Italy.

He formed a group of armed gangs called Black Shirts. The Black Shirts were mostly ex-soldiers. They violently attacked antifascist groups.

In 1922, Mussolini sent the Black Shirts to march on Rome against Italian King Victor Emmanuel II. They forced the king to make Mussolini the prime minister, the head of government.

Mussolini's Black Shirts marching in Rome

Mussolini spent the next three years building his power. In 1925, he made himself dictator. The people called him *Il Duce* (eel DOO-chay), "The Leader."

As dictator, Mussolini made all political parties except his own illegal. He put strict controls on businesses, schools, newspapers, and the police. School textbooks were

Il Duce's Propaganda

Few Italians opposed Mussolini. Fear was one of the reasons for this. Propaganda was another reason. Mussolini used propaganda to create a certain image of himself. He convinced many Italians that he was a great leader who could make Italy a powerful nation.

rewritten to glorify Mussolini and to teach fascist ideas and policies. The Black Shirts continued to harass, and even kill, people who disagreed with Mussolini's ideas.

In 1927, Mussolini set up a secret police force to spy on people. They were looking for people who were against Mussolini and his government.

Mussolini's Life

Born near Predappio, Italy	Earns teaching degree	Writes for socialist newspaper in Austria	Thrown out of Socialist Party	Fights in World War I
1883	**1901**	**1909**	**1914**	**1915–1917**

IT'S A FACT

The Black Shirts did not often use the murderous methods that the Nazis used in Germany. But they had a favorite way of dealing with people who spoke out against Mussolini. They tied these people to trees. Then the Black Shirts forced them to drink a bottle of bitter-tasting oil. This treatment usually worked to keep people quiet in the future.

Mussolini speaking to a crowd of factory workers

Becomes prime minister | **1922**

Becomes dictator | **1925**

Enters Italy into World War II | **1940**

Forced from power and imprisoned | **1943**

Shot by Italian antifascists | **1945**

Mussolini was hungry for glory. He planned to turn Italy into a major world empire. As his first step, he conquered the African country of Ethiopia in 1936. The same year, he formed an alliance with German dictator Adolf Hitler. When World War II began, Italy entered the war on Germany's side. But Italy's army and economy were not prepared for war. Mussolini's military campaigns did not go well.

In 1943, under orders from the king of Italy, the government forced Mussolini from power and put him in prison. The Germans rescued Mussolini and made him leader of German-controlled territory in northern Italy.

In 1945, German forces in Italy were being defeated in the war. Mussolini tried to escape to Switzerland, but was caught by Italians who opposed him. He was shot the next day and buried in an unmarked grave.

PRIMARY SOURCE

Benito Mussolini once said, "Here is the epitaph I want on my tomb: 'Here lies one of the most intelligent animals who ever appeared on the face of the earth.'"

Joseph Stalin

As the head of the Soviet Union, Joseph Stalin helped defeat Germany's Adolf Hitler in World War II. Stalin also helped his country become one the world's leading industrial nations. For years, many in the Soviet Union thought of him as a great leader.

But Joseph Stalin was also a brutal dictator. He caused the deaths of at least 20 million people during his 24-year reign of terror. His cruelty was based on his hunger for power and his fear of supposed "enemies." Stalin used secret police, torture, prison, and death camps to keep his people in constant fear. Eventually his methods would become known as "Stalinism."

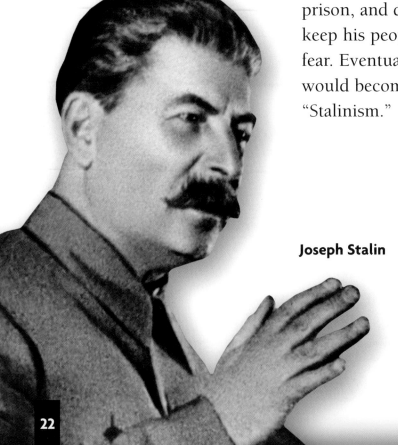

Joseph Stalin

Stalin was born on December 21, 1879. His early life was not easy. His family had very little money. His mother worked as a maid, and his father was an alcoholic who beat him. Stalin suffered from smallpox and other diseases. One disease caused his left arm to be slightly deformed.

Stalin's family lived in Georgia, a land in eastern Europe that was ruled by the czar (ZAHR), or king, of nearby Russia. The people of Georgia had no say in how they were ruled. This might have played some part in Stalin's resentment of authority. For most of his life, he disliked and distrusted people who had more power than himself.

IT'S A FACT

At different times in his life, Stalin called himself by different names. It wasn't until 1913 that he began calling himself Stalin. He chose it because it means "man of steel." He stuck with the name Stalin for the rest of his life.

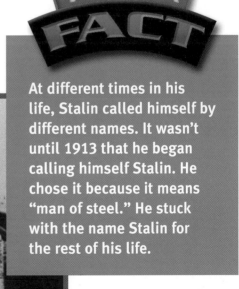

Stalin's childhood home in Georgia

Joseph Stalin as a young man

Stalin's mother was religious and ambitious. She hoped her son would become a priest. A good student, Stalin won a scholarship to a seminary, or school to train priests. But Stalin's resentment of authority caused him problems with his teachers. He was expelled from the school in 1899. Stalin never finished his education. Many of the people Stalin would later sentence to death were well educated.

Before he was expelled, Stalin and other students had joined an underground, or secret, political group. This group wanted Georgia to become independent from Russia.

The hammer and sickle were a symbol of the Soviet Union.

Stalin had found a new purpose in life—revolution. Revolution is the act of overthrowing one government and replacing it with another one. He and his friends hated the rule of the Russian czar. Most people living under the czar's rule were poor and uneducated. Eventually, Stalin joined the Bolsheviks (BOHL-shuh-vihks), a group of revolutionaries. Vladimir (VLA-deh-mir) I. Lenin was the leader of the Bolsheviks. Lenin and the Bolsheviks wanted to lead the people in overthrowing the czar.

As a revolutionary, Stalin led many marches and strikes against the Russian government. He planned robberies to raise money for revolutionary activities. He was arrested and sent to prison in Siberia, a remote area of Russia.

IT'S A FACT

The Bolsheviks based their actions on the ideas of German writer Karl Marx. Marx believed that the poor people of the working class would someday overthrow the rich people of the ruling class. He hoped for a society where wealth is shared evenly and there are no class differences. He called this communism.

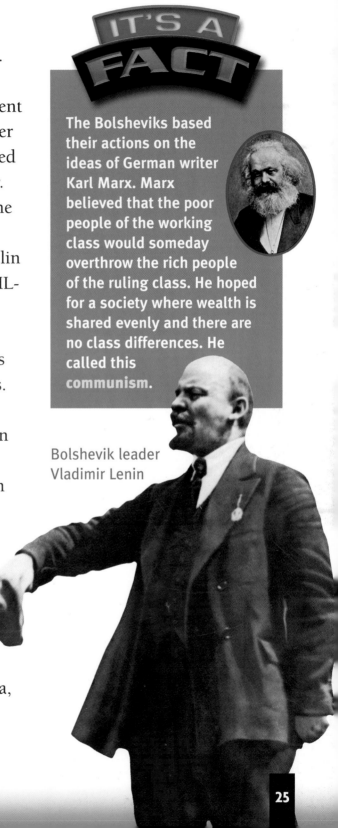

Bolshevik leader Vladimir Lenin

In 1914, Russia entered World War I to fight against Germany. Millions of Russian soldiers died. Food shortages at home led to riots and strikes. The people's anger and unrest helped the Bolsheviks with their plans for a Russian revolution. In 1917, the Bolsheviks overthrew the government.

A new government was created, with Lenin as its leader. Stalin began with a low-level government position and worked his way up. By 1922, the Bolsheviks were calling themselves the Communist Party, and Stalin had the high-level job of General Secretary. Also in 1922, Russia joined with three other territories and became known as the Soviet Union.

Meanwhile, Lenin had become suspicious that Stalin abused his power. Lenin wrote a letter, warning the party to remove Stalin from his job. But Lenin died before his wishes became known. In 1929, Stalin became dictator of the Soviet Union.

Lenin (left) and Stalin in 1922

PRIMARY SOURCE

Stalin once said, "A single death is a tragedy; a million deaths is a statistic."

The Soviet Union was far behind the United States and western Europe when it came to industry. Stalin hated that fact. He started new industries, such as steelmaking. He put many Soviet businesses under government control.

Stalin took land from hundreds of thousands of farmers. He then had the farmers and peasants who worked for them murdered or sent to prisons or brutal labor camps. He used their land to create huge collective farms. On collective farms, the government decided which crops or animals would be raised, how much the peasants would be paid for their work, and how much farmers had to give to the government.

Many farmers defied Stalin by destroying their crops and livestock. This resulted in widespread food shortages and death from starvation. As punishment, Stalin had many of these farmers killed. From the late 1920s to the early 1930s, millions of farmers and peasants died because of Stalin. But no one dared to stop him.

IT'S A FACT

Stalin used propaganda to convince the Soviet people that he was a brave leader. For example:

The Lie
Stalin was helping direct the fighting on November 7, 1917, when the Bolsheviks took over the Russian government.

The Truth
He was having tea with his fiancée and her parents.

Stalin trusted no one. He thought that even his close friends might be threats. In the mid-1930s he started what was called the Great Purge. With the help of a brutal secret police force, Stalin had about 4 million people murdered or imprisoned.

A few of Stalin's victims were probably real enemies. But many were Communist Party leaders who were probably no threat to him. Others were military officers or aides. Some were old friends. Most were ordinary citizens.

In 1939, Stalin joined forces with the German dictator Adolf Hitler to invade Poland. Then Hitler broke this partnership and invaded the Soviet Union in 1941. So Stalin switched sides. He entered the Soviet Union into World War II, fighting with the Allied forces against Germany.

Stalin (left), U.S. President Franklin D. Roosevelt, and British Prime Minister Winston Churchill met in 1943. They decided to work together to defeat Germany.

Stalin's Life

1879	1894	1898	1899	1903
Born in Gori, Georgia	Enters the seminary	Joins underground revolutionary group	Expelled from the seminary	Sent to Siberia

After World War II, Stalin broke off relations with the Allied countries. He placed several eastern European countries under Soviet control. The United States and other countries worked to block Stalin's efforts. This period of tension between democratic and communist nations became known as the "Cold War." The Cold War was not fought with troops and guns. It was fought with propaganda.

In 1953, Stalin began to prepare for another purge, or removal, of Communist Party leaders. But on March 5,

This sign from 1978 is an example of Soviet propaganda.

1953, he died suddenly, and the purge never happened. Stalin's brutal career was over, but the Cold War went on. Finally in the late 1980s, communism in eastern Europe began to collapse. In 1991, the Soviet Union itself broke into 15 independent countries.

1913
Changes name to Stalin

1929
Becomes dictator

1929
Establishes system of collective farms

1935
Begins the Great Purge

1953
Dies

Conclusion

Anti-Communists burn a picture of Stalin in 1956.

itler, Mussolini, and Stalin all came from humble beginnings. They rose to power while their countries were in crisis. They used propaganda to promote their cause. They used violence and murder to help them stay in power. They wanted absolute power that reached beyond their nations' borders. And they crushed those who disagreed with them.

Germany, Italy, and the countries of the former Soviet Union have survived the influence of these dictators. Unfortunately, many countries in crisis around the world are ruled by dictators today. In these countries, civil liberties like freedom of speech and religion do not exist and people are still executed for being critical of government policies.

Glossary

absolute power   **(AB-suh-loot POW-er) in government, the power to make all decisions alone** (page 2)

Allies   **(AL-ighz) one side that fought in World War II, including Great Britain, the United States, and the Soviet Union** (page 13)

communism   **(KAHM-yoon-ihz-uhm) a society where wealth is shared evenly and there are no class differences** (page 25)

concentration camp   **(kahn-sehn-TRAY-shuhn kamp) a large prison camp where Hitler sent Jews and other people** (page 12)

depression   **(dih-PREH-shuhn) a severe economic downturn leading to widespread unemployment and poverty** (page 11)

fascism   **(FA-shih-zuhm) a system in which all industry and labor are controlled by the government, and opposition is not allowed** (page 18)

Holocaust   **(HAHL-uh-cawst) the tragic period of mass killing of Jews and other people by Hitler** (page 13)

persecution   **(per-seh-KYOO-shuhn) abusive treatment** (page 12)

propaganda   **(prohp-uh-GAN-duh) communication designed to promote a certain cause or belief** (page 4)

socialism   **(SOH-shuhl-ihz-uhm) a system in which businesses and industries are owned or managed by the government and the people share the goods and services they produce** (page 14)

Index